TRADITIONS
IN FOLK ART

TRADITIONS IN FOLK ART

Helen Kuster

Kangaroo Press

Acknowledgments

This book was only made possible with the support of my husband Albert, the understanding of my children Egon and Ziggy, and the persistence of my many students.

It was made a great deal more pleasurable by working with the beautifully made wood pieces from Robert and Virginia Brown from Timber Turn. All of the project pieces in this book are readily available through your local stockist of Timber Turn products. The paints and mediums used are all Jo Sonja brand from Chroma Acrylics.

I have included a bibliography, but many of the books I used for inspiration are either out of print, in German, expensive, or all of the above. If you are a serious painter, finding them is well worth the trouble and expense.

Although I consider myself self-taught in the styles demonstrated in this book I have gained painting experience by working with such people as (in no particular order) Enid Hoessinger, Jan McGregor, Lyn Foster, Diana Brandt, Liz White, Ann Johnston and Scottie Foster.

Frontispiece: Round Kleister tray (see page 53)

First published in 1997 by Kangaroo Press Pty Ltd
3 Whitehall Road Kenthurst NSW 2156 Australia
PO Box 6125 Dural Delivery Centre NSW 2158
Printed in Hong Kong through Colorcraft Ltd

ISBN 0 86417 860 3

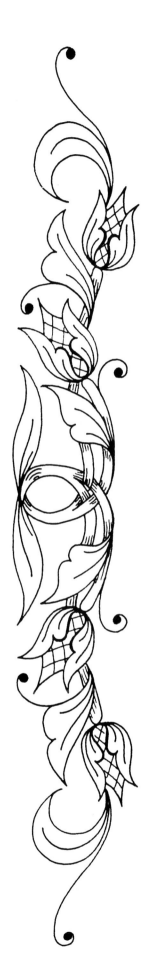

CONTENTS

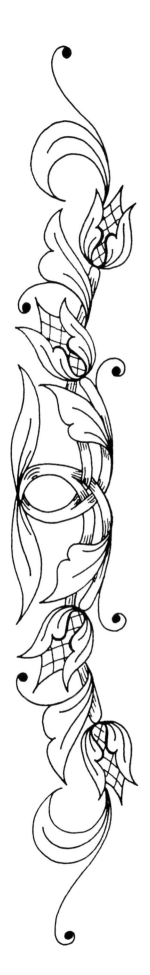

FOREWORD

Traditions in Folk Art has been written for folk art enthusiasts with some painting experience. If you are a beginner, having never painted before, I recommend you read and work through *The Rustic Charm of Folk Art* by Diana Brandt, which will get you started with many techniques and lots of information.

I have tried to include as much detailed information as possible without duplicating too much of the information already available. A short note at the start of each project gives you a little history where applicable and some idea of the level of difficulty involved, or the patience required to complete the project. Please take the time to read through the information on tools and techniques at the beginning of the book, and all the instructions for an individual project, before you start.

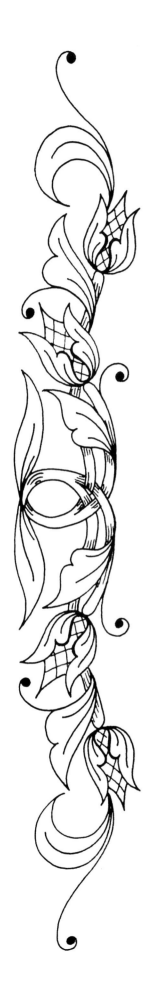

history

I have always been interested in the history behind folk art and try to be as traditional as possible in my work without compromising the results. Because some of my methods may seem at first glance to be a little odd or messy, a short background history will help to explain them.

There are as many versions of the history of folk art as there are people who are experts on the subject. Because it was originally a peasant art (and I am now speaking mainly about Central Europe) there is no documentation of its beginnings—all we have are the surviving pieces and the odd book written long after it began. After researching the subject one can surmise much of the history, without being too dogmatic about it (you can always come across another version that changes your opinion).

The first folk artists were not trained as artists. They were craftsmen or farmers who wanted to copy the expensive decorated furniture fashionable among the merchant and upper classes, which was mostly inlaid wood. The folk artists had access to stencils, devised by inlay workers and other artisans, which they used in numerous ways to create designs imitating inlay work. The wood at this stage was not base-painted, merely sealed. The stencil was laid on the wood and the design stencilled on. Where a negative stencil was used for the background, leaving flowers and foliage bare, colour was then painted free-hand onto the design areas and strokes added later.

I have painted most of my work using fairly watery paint, not because it was the traditional method but because it simulates an aged faded effect. For the same reason I have often sealed the wood with a yellow background; when the wood is antiqued I get an aged mellow look similar to the old pieces. Antiquing is not a traditional technique, but it is the quickest way I know to simulate two hundred years of dirt and mellowing of natural wood. Some early folk artists did use a coloured glaze over their finished work that muted the colours.

Folk art was widely accepted and it became a tradition to give hand-painted bedroom furniture when a couple married; often the names of the recipients were painted on the furniture.

Stylised Renaissance designs evolved into the busier, freer designs of the Baroque and then on to the Rococo, when background colours started to appear, heavy scroll and shell forms were used to frame large designs, and religious symbols and pictures appeared.

Varying styles, palettes and traditions are evident from the different regions. Depending on geographic location, influences from many different sources are identifiable. I have seen early Swiss clocks with what appear to be Dutch

Hindeloopen tulips painted among the usual Swiss flowers. Regions on trade routes or close to cities were exposed to many more influences than the isolated valleys.

Trying to slot old pieces into a style period can become quite confusing; many folk artists continued working in the stylised Renaissance manner well into the Rococo period, just adding the odd Rococo scroll or shell form (as in the Alpbachtal medicine cupboard on page 57). In fact, some historians claim that folk art ended when true Rococo designs began to be painted, with their three-dimensional scroll effects and lush realistic roses. As folk art became more complex and challenging it is reasonable to surmise that some formally trained artists also turned to painting furniture.

In those days it was traditional to paint only exotic flowers—roses, tulips or carnations. Local wildflowers are very rarely seen. Even after the use of stencils was abandoned, the flower forms remained stilted, often constructed using compass and ruler. Many of them are pure fantasy. The use of strokework to create shadows and highlights is a strong tradition, and although by our standards the strokework was often very rough and poorly done, when viewed as a whole the designs were very effective.

Throughout the projects in this book I have used strokework, and the extra effects gained by antiquing. I have designed my patterns following the traditional notion of filling up all available space with flowers, leaves, striping or strokes.

The Kleister techniques seem to crop up in any period, the designs changing to suit the prevailing fashion. Kleister is very versatile, and I have taken it a step further in the brass rubbing box and the Art Nouveau lap desk on pages 32 and 47.

My Kleister techniques are not always standard. I have found that masking film in many cases gives me a better, quicker, easier result than using the traditional stencils, especially in complex designs like the fire screen on page 50. The small rectangular Kleister box on page 22 comes closest to the traditional Kleister technique. The original Kleister medium would have been made up of flour and water paste, often coloured with the dye extracted from ground walnut shells, but using commercial Kleister medium and paint suits me fine!

I hope that through painting the projects in this book you will get a feel for traditional folk art and go on to create projects of your own. It is always best to go back to the original works if you wish to study traditional folk art. Any modern design, even though inspired by historical pieces, is a modern artist's intepretation of the original style. I very rarely copy the old designs exactly as I enjoy creating new designs using the old subjects. Most of the projects in this book are thus my interpretations of traditional designs—for me that is what folk art is all about.

Helen Kuster

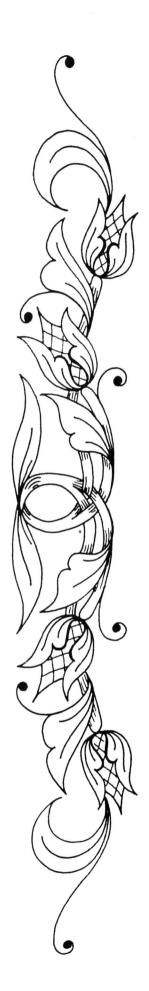

GLOSSARY OF STYLES

Folk art styles were defined using names common to art and architecture—Renaissance, Baroque and Rococo—and by geographic areas, as in Alpbachtal. Folk art doesn't necessarily reflect the styles in art and architecture; the names are used more to place folk art chronologically.

RENAISSANCE (FOLK ART): 16TH AND 17TH CENTURIES

A very simple stylised portrayal of flowers, fruit and birds painted or stencilled on an unpainted background.

ALPBACHTAL

A Renaissance style of folk art painted in the region of the Tyrol in Austria. It was centred around a valley called Alpbach and used a very simple palette and included flowers, birds and animals.

BAROQUE (FOLK ART): LATE 17TH–MID 18TH CENTURIES

This style bridges the gap between Renaissance and Rococo, still using stylised elements. It is looser than the Renaissance style, and shows more flowing designs; later it starts to show the fussy curls and scrolls of Rococo.

ROCOCO (FOLK ART): MID 18TH–EARLY 19TH CENTURIES

The backgrounds are now base-coated, usually in blue or green. Large heavy shell and scroll forms and less styled fruit, flowers and birds; heavy use of marbling techniques and bright striping.

ART NOUVEAU: EARLY 20TH CENTURY

This style was used extensively in interior decoration and architecture, together with Art Deco (a style based on geometric design). Art Nouveau was based on organic growth forms; the designs appear simple and flowing, with design elements often weaving through the overall design.

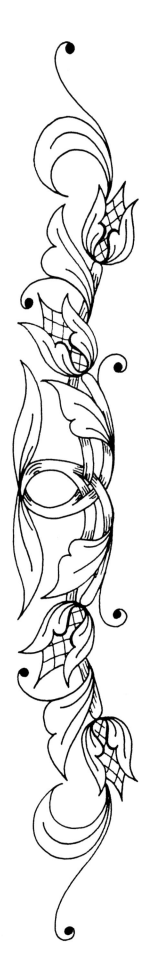

Tools & Techniques

The information in this section on tools and techniques is meant as a guide only. Always experiment first with what you have: in Australia we have so many different climates that what works well in one area may be a disaster in another. It is always worthwhile trying out new products and techniques but never be afraid to adapt them for your own situation and requirements.

BRUSHES

For strokework throughout the book I have specified either a No. 4 or a No. 2 round brush (acrylic) and a No. 2 liner brush (acrylic). My personal favourite in a round brush is the Raphael sable series 8404, No. 2, which is a very full brush and around the same size as most acrylic No. 4 rounds; the No. 1 in this series is the equivalent of a No. 2 acrylic round. Since I first started painting folk art I have used the Raphael acrylic No. 2 liner brush; I have tried many others but always come back to this one.

The flat brushes used here are for striping, base-coating, or applying mediums, so old ones are fine.

The hogshair brush I use for Kleister wood-graining, which has stiff white hairs, is readily available from art and craft shops very cheaply.

CUTTING KNIVES AND MATS

The cutting knife I prefer has a round handle and a replaceable sharp-angled blade. The round handle makes the knife comfortable to use—you can roll it slightly between your fingers to cut around small curves. Most craft shops or art suppliers have a range of knives.

The most satisfactory cutting mat is the green self-healing mat often used by patchwork quilters. The surface is slightly soft and cuts don't permanently damage it. A well-worn wooden chopping board can be a problem when cutting a fine stencil, as the knife can slip into an old cut on the board and be withdrawn only with great difficulty. Damage to the stencil is the usual result.

FRISK FILM

Frisk film, sold for artists, is also called masking film. I always buy it in the matt format but it is also available in gloss. Frisk film is less tacky than Contact film, a plus when it has to remain on your work for some time. Contact film can be very sticky and may leave a layer of glue behind when you lift it off.

A few precautions must be taken when using frisk film: never use a hairdryer over it, or leave it on your work in the sun or in a warm place, as the glue softens readily and may stay on your work. Film placed over a metallic colour or left on the work for long periods (more than four to six days) must be lifted off especially carefully as it can pull paint off. Film is a very useful material for replacing a stencil, especially where a design is so complex a stencil could fall apart or requires the use of a multi-layer stencil.

STENCIL MATERIAL

Any material you use to cut a stencil must be reasonably waterproof, otherwise when you apply the paint it will buckle or disintegrate. I like to use drafting film for stencils; it blunts my blades fairly quickly but is not as brittle as acetate film and is therefore stronger, especially for fine stencils or a stencil I want to use many times. X-ray film can also be used, but as it is fairly tough I would not recommend using it for a complex stencil that needs a lot of cutting.

TRANSFER EQUIPMENT

This means graphite paper and stylus. I use grey or black graphite paper whenever I can, using white only when the background is really dark. I have had students replace graphite paper with a variety of other transferable products, most of which have ended up causing problems, some of them disastrous. I always use a stylus to transfer the design onto the work—do not press too hard as you may bruise the wood. Bruising can show up when you antique a project, especially on pine.

PAINT

Throughout the book I have used Jo Sonja paints. These paints suit the way I work and are very strong; I can water them down for very fine work, or antique over them and rub over them without their disappearing. Other brands may need a coat of glaze before antiquing to protect liner work.

WOOD

Nothing beats using good quality wood as the base for these projects—poor wood can ruin a beautifully painted project.

Craftwood is ideal to work with the frisk film technique—there is no grain for your knife to get stuck in, and it has to be base-painted anyway. Beware of poor quality craftwood, which can pose problems when you are using frisk film—the film can lift off layers of wood. Poor quality pine can 'grab' antiquing so that you end up with a patchy finish.

When choosing a technique for a piece I keep to the general rule that if the piece is pine I will paint in such a way that the grain remains visible.

SANDING & BASE-COATING

If the piece is pine I sand it automatically before doing anything else, while craftwood I sand after the first coat of base-paint has dried. The sandpaper I use has a white surface and really cuts into an uneven surface without clogging up the paper or glazing the surface of the wood. For rough sanding or a distressed finish I use 180 grade; if the wood is good, 240 grade for the first couple of sands. I always finish with 320 grade before I transfer the design.

Always base-paint in one direction, with the grain on pine and with the length on craftwood. The number of coats you need will depend on the consistency of the paint. When a project calls for one base-coat on pine do not use too much water, otherwise the wood will not be properly sealed and will bleed when you paint the design on. Sand each coat of base-paint when it's dry.

GLAZING

A transparent glaze medium mixed with paint can be used as a stain on pine or to paint over a base-coated surface for different techniques. To make a stain mix enough paint into the glaze medium to give the colour you want, and roughly base the well-sanded pine with this mix, wiping off the excess with a soft cloth. On large projects complete one surface at a time for an even finish. I usually use half paint, half glaze medium. Glaze medium can be painted onto delicate work to protect it before antiquing.

TRACING & TRANSFERRING DESIGNS

Note: Some of the designs have had to be reduced to fit on the page. Whenever possible enlarge by photocopying and join the pattern pieces together. Use the percentage enlargement noted on the patterns to fit the pieces shown in this book.

Always trace the *full* design onto transparent paper first. Where only half a design is given, make a tracing-paper pattern of the exact surface size of your project, *then* trace the design on the paper twice so you have the full pattern. Transferring one half of a design onto the work, then trying to fit on the second half, can often cause more problems than the time lost tracing onto the paper twice.

The designs indicate the colours required and suggest the strokework on only one portion of the pattern. Do not transfer the colour indications or the strokework onto your tracing. Strokework is a personal touch and should be done freehand.

STROKEWORK

Traditional folk art is a showcase for strokework. With practice, using strokes is a relatively quick painting method. Use your natural strokes whenever possible.

When basing in flowers, leaves and detail use shape-following strokes. Everyone's natural strokes are different, so the main shapes, which were designed for my strokes, may not always be abso-

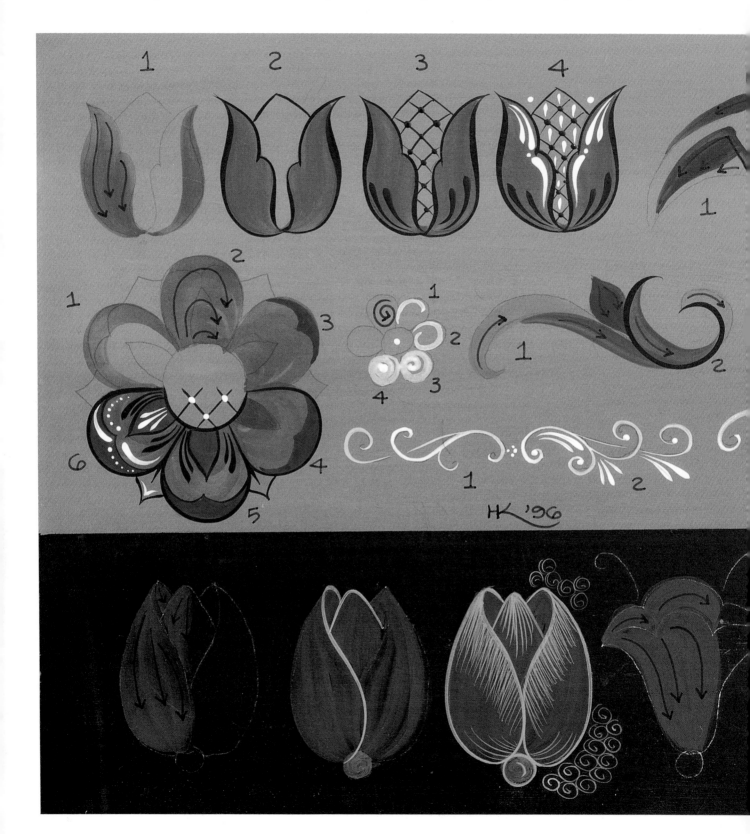

lutely comfortable for you to paint. The details and extra strokes indicated on the patterns are only a guide and show what I have painted.

RENAISSANCE & ALPBACHER FLOWERS

Yellow area

Renaissance tulip (top left)
1. Starting at the tip of the petal, using shape-following strokes, base in the tulip with a No. 4 round brush.
2. Using liner brush and ink-consistency paint outline tulip petals.
3. Add all the dark detail using a liner brush.
4. Add the textured white detail with the liner brush.

Renaissance rose (bottom left)
1. Using No. 4 round brush and C strokes, base in the full rose petal using red.
2. Several C strokes are used to fill in the full petal.
3. The dark red turn on the petal is painted in using a No. 2 round brush.
4. Using green on a No. 2 round brush, paint in the leaves, using blue paint in the centre petal. With the liner brush and dark paint outline all elements.
5. Now add all the dark detail with a liner brush.
6. Using a liner brush add the white detail with texture.

Alpbacher flowers (top right)
1. Using a round brush and following the arrows base in the flowers and leaves. Use shape-following strokes wherever possible. The leaves on these designs are quite angular and our natural strokes don't always fit easily.
2. Outline all elements using liner brush and ink-consistency paint.
3. Add the white detail with a liner brush. The fine lines on the large leaf are watery; all the other white detail is textured.

Small white daisy (middle left)
1. Using watery white paint and the tip of a No. 4 round brush start on the outside edge of the petal.
2. Go all the way around the outside.
3. When you meet up the start of this stroke keep going in ever smaller circles until the petal is more or less covered.
4. Add a textured white dot in the centre of each petal and the centre of the daisy.

Renaissance leaves and buds (middle right)
1. Using round brush and shape-following strokes base in all areas.
2. Outline in dark paint using liner brush and ink-consistency paint.
3. Add any dark detail using a liner brush, then white detail with a liner brush. The white in the leaves is watery and remaining detail is textured.

Renaissance border details (bottom centre and right)
1. Using a liner brush and watery white paint, paint in the curls that you have transferred onto your work.
2. Still using white and the liner brush, texture the extra commas and dots. This looks quite flat until antiquing, when the watery strokes become a soft dirty white and the textured strokes come back white, giving a much more interesting look.

Black area

Closed tulip (left)
1. Base in red using a round brush and shape-following strokes.
2. Add green calyx and outline all petals using a liner brush and ink-consistency yellow paint.
3. Add very fine yellow detail using a liner brush. Background is filled up with watery white liner brush curls.

Open tulip (right)
1. Base in red using a round brush, following arrows.
2. Base calyx in green; outline tulip in white using liner brush.
3. Add very fine white liner brush detail and white dots. The calyx and top curls are painted yellow with a liner brush. Paint background curls in watery white with a liner brush.

STENCILLING

The use of stencils was one of the original folk art techniques. They are particularly useful if you want to paint a number of pieces with the same design. Refer to the notes on stencil materials on page 13. The design is traced onto the material using a permanent pen to prevent smudging. Always cut the smallest areas of a stencil first, and the outside edge shape last. Try to pull single cuts from point to point, working from an uncut point to a cut point whenever possible to minimise the risk of tearing. When the stencil is cut and ready to position I spray a very light coat of spray adhesive on the back, just enough to hold it in place but not so much that glue will be left on the work when the stencil is lifted. This way you have two hands free to paint with. Use a virtually dry brush with minimal paint and a pouncing motion; too much paint or too wet a mix and the paint will seep under the stencil and ruin the effect. Lift the stencil only when you have finished, and lift it carefully so it does not rip.

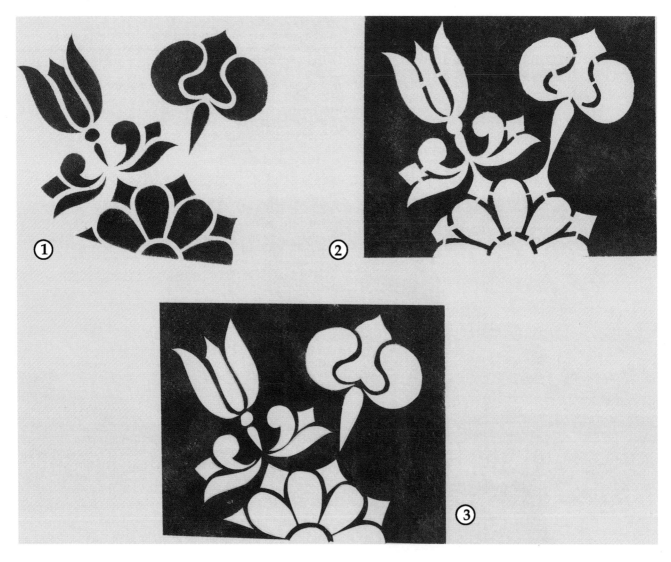

1. Positive stencil On this stencil the stencil material remained over the background of the design (the light area). The separated petals of the flowers hold the stencil together. This technique is used on the small rectangular Kleister box on page 22.

2. Negative stencil The stencil material on this design is the flowers and leaves (light-coloured). This creates a more broken effect as 'bridges' must be made in the design to hold the stencil together while the background is painted.

3. Masking film stencil By using masking film that is firmly stuck to the painted surface a positive stencil design can be used for a negative stencil effect. Because the film is fixed to the work before cutting you don't have to worry about the stencil falling apart. This technique is very good for small intricate designs such as the brass rubbing box on page 32 and for designs where wood-graining techniques are used instead of stencilling in backgrounds, such as the fire screen on page 50.

16

POSITIVE AND NEGATIVE STENCILS

Positive stencil The design elements are cut out of the stencil material. When the stencil is used it is the design elements that are painted onto the surface.

Negative stencil The background is cut out of the stencil material. When the stencil is used on a surface the design remains the existing surface colour and the background is painted.

ANTIQUING

Antiquing, not a traditional technique, mellows new work to give it an aged look, and can be played with to give designs extra depth. You will need soft cotton cloths, an old brush (I use a 25 mm/1" housepaint brush), cotton buds, patina and oil paints. The patina can be purchased ready mixed or you can make your own from four parts gum turps to one part linseed oil. The oil paints should be artist's oils, as lesser quality paint can be difficult to work with and can spoil the end result. Only a relatively small amount of oil paint is necessary, so I feel the extra cost is worth it.

Squeeze a few chocolate chip sized dots of oil paint over the surface to be antiqued (to give you a guide, four or five dots on the lap desk lid), and spread this around roughly. Pour a small amount of patina into a small dish, dip the brush into it and use it to work the oil evenly over the surface. (It's a good idea to experiment with the quantities on a practice surface first; you can always add more oil paint at the start of the process, but too much is a waste, while too much patina will remove all the oil paint.) Using the cloth with a circular motion, rub the surface to an even soft coverage, rubbing a little more in the centre for extra glow if you like.

When I want extra shadow, as in the fire screen on page 50, I use the barest touch of patina, if any. Work with the cloth for even coverage, then using cotton buds and a little extra patina if needed, rub in highlights. On the fire screen I added extra oil paint to the shadows as well, blending it in with a soft cloth; this gives the same effect that the inlay artists achieved by plunging wood into hot sand to softly scorch areas of the design they wanted slightly darker.

When I work on boxes or cupboards I antique one surface at a time, then spray it with a fixative spray so my fingerprints will not mar the completed surface while I work on the next side.

The finished work must then be left to cure properly for one or two weeks before varnishing or waxing, the length of time depending on climatic conditions.

WARNING

Patina and oil paint can be a dangerous mix; although each by itself is safe, together they they can self-combust. After you have finished antiquing dispose of used rags and contaminated patina very carefully. Never return used patina to the bottle, as it will always have some oil paint in it from your brush. Collect all the rags and cotton buds with antiquing mix in them, soak up all the contaminated patina from the dish and wipe it dry, then place the rags and cotton buds in a plastic bag. Pour water over the rags, squeeze the water through them and tie off the bag after pressing out as much of the air as you can. This effectively drowns and suffocates the rags. Put the plastic bag in an outdoor rubbish bin, away from combustible materials—just in case.

The brush can be kept soft and ready to use by standing it in a jar of water which should be kept regularly topped up. Squeeze out excess water when you are ready to use it again.

A Complete wood-grain panel
This panel shows a finished wood-grain. The angle of this panel's grain is correct in relation to the panel next to it, i.e. all panels have grains running straight from the centre of the project.

B Wood-grain panel in progress
1. *Mask around area to be wood-grained.*
2. *Roughly base in area with Kleister and paint mix.*
3. *With the hogshair brush, starting in the centre of the area and working from masking tape to edge, pull a straight grain. All the grains will now follow this first stroke. Grain the whole area then remove the masking tape.*

C A variety of finishes
Base in Kleister/paint mix then choose your pattern technique:
1. *Twisting a stencil brush, overlapping the twists.*
2. *Using your finger make a small circular motion, slightly overlapping swirls.*
3. *Crumple up some newspaper and dab onto wet based area.*

D Detail of fire screen *(refer to page 50)*
Left side: *After stage 1 is completed; the background has been wood-grained, the first part of the design transferred has been covered with film and so remains the background colour.*
Right side: *A completed portion. The rest of the design has been transferred and painted in according to the instructions, on top of the wood-grain background.*

KLEISTER TECHNIQUE

The terms 'Kleister' and 'intarsia' can be confusing. Kleister is the technique of wood-graining, while intarsia refers to inlaid work which may sometimes involve the use of Kleister techniques. Kleister is also the name given to the paste used in the early wood-graining techniques and to the medium we now use. Kleister medium added to paint allows you to create a pattern in the paint that will remain after the paint is dry. It also makes the paint transparent—the more medium in your mix the more transparent it becomes, allowing the base colour to glow through. I usually use a yellow base to give a natural wood glow. The Kleister projects in this book have been painted with a variety of yellow bases to give you some variety to go on and experiment with.

If the Kleister technique is going to be used over all surfaces of a project, good base-coat coverage is not needed, as in the small and medium rectangular boxes on pages 22 and 26. If some of the design areas will not be covered by the Kleister, good base-coat coverage is essential, as on the lap desk, fire screen and round tray on pages 47, 50 and 53.

I keep my different Kleister colours ready mixed in small airtight containers. In very dry conditions or where you are painting large areas, a few drops of retarder in the mix will make it easier to use.

Basic Kleister technique is to roughly cover the base-coated surface with the mix, then to drag a textured object though it to create a pattern. Try rolled-up terry towelling, a variety of brushes, cardboard or plastic with jagged 'teeth' cut into one edge, paper towel, sponges, your fingers dabbed or swirled, or use a stylus. Where a fine wood-grain is called for you will need to wipe excess mix off your brush or tool from time to time to prevent ridges forming; a smooth surface is needed when stencilling over a wood grain or when a second layer of Frisk film needs to be placed over it. I have used Kleister as a background in the Medium Kleister and Renaissance box on pages 26.

WAXING AND VARNISHING

Waxing and/or varnishing gives a final glow to the colours of the finished work. I prefer a waxed finish, and only use varnish when I have to, as with the tray on page 53. Waxing can give textured light-coloured strokework an extra dimension; the wire wool will remove the antiquing from raised areas, bringing them back to the original colour. A simple white comma after waxing can look as though it was painted in two colours, the tail a brown-white and the head pure white.

Waxing is a straightforward process. Using a mixture of beeswax and gum turps the consistency of soft butter, I apply a thin smear to all surfaces with a soft cloth, then remove the excess and buff up using 000 steel wool in a circular motion. You will know you have removed all excess wax when a clean piece of steel wool glides smoothly over the surface. A final buff using a piece of lambswool completes the process. If the item is well used you can always give it another waxing when the surface becomes dull.

Varnishing is necessary on projects such as the round tray on which hot cups will be placed. Of course, all the projects can be varnished if you prefer. You can buff with steel wool before varnishing the strokework projects to achieve the same effect as I have with waxing; just be sure to clean all surfaces well before you varnish.

A solvent-based varnish is needed on antiqued work, while a water-based one can be used on projects that have not been antiqued. For both varnishes I use a soft mop brush and plenty of varnish and gently float the varnish on, always pulling from the centre toward the edge to prevent too many drips. Wipe up any drips as you go along.

Solvent-based varnishes need a fair time to dry so a dust- and fluff-free workspace is needed. Do not varnish in the same area where you sand or work with wire wool. It is also best not to wear knitted clothing while you are varnishing, as the fibres have a habit of falling out onto the work or into the varnish! Several coats of varnish can be applied, sanding and cleaning the surface after each coat. Only a light sanding is required, leaving at least a day between each coat for safety. A second coat on a sanded coat within the same day can crackle the first one. (It's happened to me!) A varnished surface can be waxed later for that same glow, but never varnish a previously waxed surface—it will not bond.

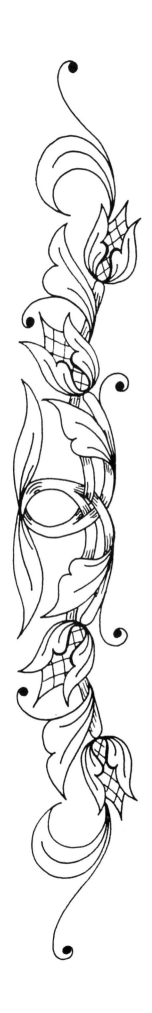

THE
PROJECTS

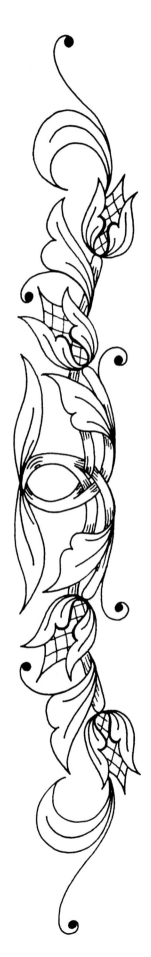

SMALL RECTANGULAR KLEISTER BOX

Illustrated on page 25
Pattern on page 60

This box is a good introduction to Kleister and stencil work. The techniques required are very straightforward and the stencil is not too fine. It makes a lovely masculine gift.

Tools
Small rectangular craftwood box,
    15 cm x 6.5 cm x 4.5 cm (6" x 2½"
    x 1¾" approx.)
Stencil material
Cutting mat and knife
Sandpaper
Base-coat brush
Newspaper
Stencil brush
Permanent marker
Beeswax
Spray glue

Paints and mediums
Yellow Oxide
Burnt Sienna
Kleister Medium
Burnt Umber

Base-coat all surfaces in Yellow Oxide and sand smooth. One or two coats will be enough as all surfaces will have a layer of Burnt Sienna Kleister over the top. Allow to dry. Trace stencil design onto stencil material using a permanent marker. Cut the three stencils, referring to stencil notes on page 16 before you begin.

Mix the Burnt Sienna and Kleister Medium in equal parts. Working on one surface at a time, roughly paint each surface with this mix, then press crumpled newspaper into the wet mix, wiping up any drips that might stray onto adjoining surfaces. All the surfaces are treated this way except for the small edge around the lid (inside and out).

Sand lightly all over, as a too-textured surface will allow stencil paint to seep under the edges of the stencil and give a fuzzy edge to the design.

Lightly spray-glue the stencils and position carefully on the lid and sides of the box.

Now you are ready to stencil on layers of Burnt Umber, always allowing the previous coat to dry before applying the next one. Keep stencilling until you have a solid Burnt Umber design.

The trim around the lid is painted in Burnt Umber.

Give the box a final light sand for a smoother finish; some texture will remain around the edge of the stencil design. It's not possible to remove all texture without damaging the painted surface.

Wax the box and it's finished.

SMALL OVAL KLEISTER BOX

Illustrated on page 24
Pattern on page 61

This a lovely simple project which uses a technique similar to that used on the small rectangular Kleister box on page 22. The preparatory work for this a little different, as this box is pine.

Tools
Small oval pine box, 9 cm x 6 cm x 3.5 cm
   (3½" x 2¼" x 1½" approx.)
Stencil material
Permanent marker
Cutting knife
Base-coat brush
Plastic wrap
Spray glue
Hogshair flat brush
No. 2 liner brush
Antiquing equipment
Burnt Sienna oil paint
Beeswax

Paints and mediums
All-Purpose Sealer
Burnt Umber
Burgundy
Kleister Medium
Carbon Black

Sand the box well, especially the cut edges, coat all surfaces with All-Purpose Sealer and lightly sand when dry.

Transfer the stencil design onto the stencil material using a permanent marker.

Cut the stencil for the top and the sides of the box, referring to the stencil notes on page 16 before you

begin. Note that this is a negative stencil.

Mix together 2 parts Kleister medium to 1 part each Burnt Umber and Burgundy.

Lightly spray-glue the stencil and position carefully on the lid and sides. Press the stencils down firmly, especially around the sides of the box.

LEFT: *Small oval Kleister box (page 23)*

especially around the sides of the box.

On all the outside surfaces except the lid band, gently dab on the Kleister mix, using crumpled plastic wrap, until the background is evenly covered with a mottled effect. Allow to dry.

The lid band is painted in small sections with Kleister mix, with the hogshair brush pulled down through the mix while it's still wet to give a vertical grained effect. Allow to dry. Carefully lift off the stencil material.

Using the liner brush and Carbon Black, outline and detail the stencilled design, following the pattern, to create the 'woven' effect.

Antique the box and wax when cured.

RIGHT: *Small rectangular Kleister box (page 22)*

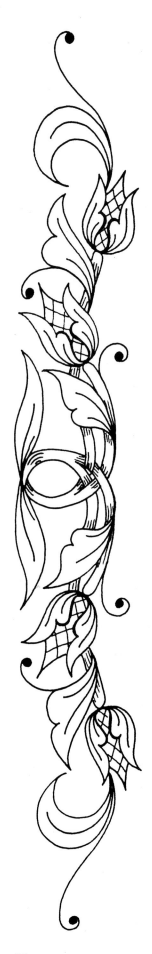

MEDIUM RECTANGULAR KLEISTER & RENAISSANCE TULIP BOX

Illustrated on page 28
Pattern on page 62

This box uses a Renaissance design and colours with a Kleister wood-grain background, a useful way to disguise craftwood. The strokework on this box needs a bit of patience because it's relatively small.

Tools
Medium sized rectangular craftwood
    box, 19.5 cm x 8.5 cm x 6.5 cm
    (7¾" x 3¼" x 2½" approx.)
Base-coat brush
Rough hogshair flat brush
White graphite paper
Stylus
No. 4 round brush (or equivalent)
No. 2 liner brush
Antiquing equipment
Burnt Umber oil paint
Varnish or wax

Paints and mediums
Yellow Light
Burnt Sienna
Kleister Medium
Green Oxide (=G)
Yellow Oxide (=Y)
Ultramarine (=B)
Naphthol Crimson (=R)
Brown Earth
Burnt Umber
Titanium White

Base-coat all surfaces in one coat of Yellow Light and sand smooth.

Mix Kleister medium and Burnt Sienna in equal parts. The outside of the box is all straight wood-grain. Working one side at a time, roughly base in with the mix and use the hogshair brush to scrape through the mix to create a grain. The inside of the box is scumbled using a flat brush and the mix. Allow to dry.

Transfer the designs onto the box.

Using shape-following strokes, the No. 4 round brush and slightly watery paint for no texture, base in the colours noted on the pattern, starting with the green, then yellow, blue and finally red.

Wash Brown Earth over the wood-grain around the arch shapes on the sides so the insides of the arches are lighter than the rest of the area.

Using the No. 2 liner brush and Burnt Umber, outline all the design elements, the detail in the centres of the tulips on the lid, and the centre of the lid pattern, adding dots to the ends of the curls.

All remaining strokework is in Titanium White. Make the paint watery for the edge designs and detail lines, but texture the commas and dots.

Paint the lid trim in Burnt Umber.

Allow to cure and either brush or spray varnish with an oil-based varnish.

MEDIUM OVAL RENAISSANCE BOX

Illustrated on page 28
Pattern on page 63

This colourful little box is worked in the most basic Renaissance technique, although working on such a small piece makes it a little more dificult. (You may wish to enlarge the pattern and try it on a bigger box first.) The swag design around the edge of the box comes originally from Greek art and was used by the early folk artists before it became popular in other forms during the Empire period.

Tools
Medium oval pine box, 11.5 cm x 7.5 cm x 5.5 cm (4½″ x 3″ x 2¼″ approx.)
Grey graphite paper
Stylus
No. 2 liner brush
No. 2 round brush (or equivalent)
No. 4 round brush (or equivalent)
Eraser
Antiquing equipment
Burnt Umber oil paint
Beeswax

Paints and mediums
All-Purpose Sealer
Carbon Black
Titanium White (= TW)
Ultra Blue Deep (= UBD)
Naphthol Crimson (= R)
Green Oxide (= G)
Glaze Medium

Sand the box and apply a coat of All-Purpose Sealer, sanding lightly when dry.

TOP LEFT: *Medium rectangular Kleister and Renaissance tulip box (page 26)*

LOWER LEFT: *Medium oval Renaissance box (page 27)*

RIGHT: *Large oval Alpbachtal box (page 30)*

Transfer the pattern onto the top and sides of the box with the grey graphite paper. Leave the band untouched. All the Carbon Black outlining and detailing is painted now with the liner brush, even the detail inside the leaves and flowers and the lines in the border pattern. Allow to dry.

The colours are now washed in over the detail strokes in watery paint so the detail is still visible. Wash the colours in according to the pattern in the following order—Titanium White, Ultra Blue Deep, Naphthol Crimson, Green Oxide—using the No. 2 round brush for small areas, and the No. 4 for the remainder. Allow to dry.

Remove any visible graphite lines with the eraser and apply a coat of glaze medium to prevent the antiquing grabbing unevenly in the wood-grain.

Paint in the Titanium White dots and commas with texture in straight paint, following the pattern and the photograph.

The band around the lid of the box is finger-rubbed in dark green (Green Oxide and Carbon Black mixed to the depth of colour you want). When dry, decorate the band, using very watery Titanium White and the liner brush, with groups of three vertical lines close together. Inside each segment paint thin white horizontal lines and groups of three dots top and bottom. Allow to dry.

Antique with Burnt Umber oil paint and wax when cured.

LARGE OVAL ALPBACHTAL BOX

Illustrated on page 29
Pattern on page 64

This design is based on a nineteenth century piece from the region of the Tyrol in Austria. Most of the pieces I have seen from this region are painted in this simple palette of red and dark green. This is not a difficult project.

Tools
Large oval pine box, 15 cm x 10.5 cm x 6.5 cm
  (6" x 4¼" x 2½" approx.)
Base-coat brush
Grey graphite paper
Stylus
No. 2 round brush (or equivalent)
No. 4 round brush (or equivalent)
No. 2 liner brush
Soft cloth
Antiquing equipment
Burnt Umber oil paint
Beeswax

Paints and mediums
Glaze Medium
Burnt Sienna
Carbon Black
Green Oxide
Ultramarine
Naphthol Crimson
Yellow Oxide
Titanium White

Green mix = 4 parts Carbon Black + 1½ parts Green Oxide + just enough Ultramarine to soften the colour without seeing the blue.

Red mix = Naphthol Crimson + Yellow Oxide; the proportions are your choice, but keep the mix red, not orange.

Sand the box well. Mix glaze medium and Burnt Sienna in equal parts and glaze all surfaces inside and out, referring to notes on glazing on page 13.

Using the red mix really washy, paint in all the red areas on the top and sides of the box so the wood grain shows through. Using the green mix, paint in all the green areas, including the lid band and the base of the box. The green is stronger than the red, not so transparent. The centres of the tulip flowers are not painted. Use the No. 2 round for the small areas and the No. 4 round for the remaining areas, e.g. the deer.

Paint the eyes and antlers in Titanium White with the No. 2 round.

Outline all design elements using the liner brush and Carbon Black and add black detail, referring to the photograph where necessary.

Now add the white detail with the liner brush. The thin detail lines on the border and on the leaves are painted using watery Titanium White. The dots and commas are textured, painted in straight Titanium White. The little flowers on the lid and base borders have a Titanium White dot centre and red mix dots for the petals.

Antique with Burnt Umber oil paint and wax when cured.

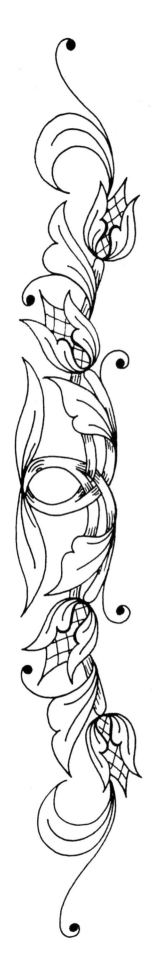

BRASS RUBBING BOX

Pattern on page 66

I had the idea for this box in mind for quite a while. The knight is based on a brass rubbing of Sir John de Creke (1325), which was 168 cm (66") long in the original. The rest of the design is my own stencilled invention. This was a fairly intense project involving a lot of cutting, but I think the end result was worth the trouble.

Tools
Long rectangular craftwood box,
   24.5 cm x 10.5 cm x 8 cm
   (9½" x 4" x 3" approx.)
Base-coat brush
Grey and white graphite paper
Stylus
Frisk or masking film
Cutting knife
Sandpaper
No. 2 liner brush
Cotton buds
Burnt Sienna oil paint

Paints and mediums
Titanium White
Yellow Oxide
Turners Yellow
Burgundy
Burnt Umber
Rich Gold

Pale yellow mix = 2 parts Titanium White + 1 part Yellow Oxide + 1 part Turners Yellow + enough Burgundy to warm the yellow without making it apricot.

Base-coat all surfaces inside and outside in pale yellow mix and sand smooth. As not all the yellow is covered at the end, a complete coverage of several coats is needed. Put a small amount of the mix aside in an airtight container for later detail work.

Transfer the pattern onto the box, except for the internal details of the knight, the shield and the dog at his feet. Lay pieces of frisk film cut to size over the top of the lid and on each of the four sides of the box. Following the photograph and the pattern, cut the film to mask out all the yellow detail (the silhouette around the knight and the arched frame, the floral decoration outside the frame, and the arched pattern and floral decoration on the sides of the box). Lift off the film from all the areas to be painted brown and burnish the remaining film down really well with your thumbnail or a burnishing tool (like a stiff mini-spatula), being very

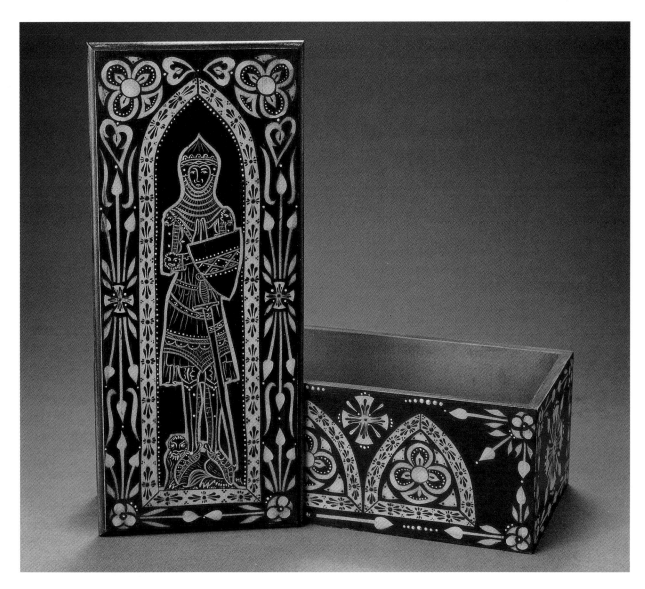

careful in the small detail areas as the film can shift.

Paint all the outside surfaces of the box in straight Burnt Umber (no water), using gentle strokes to prevent paint being forced under the film.

Allow to dry, and very carefully lift away the film. Lightly sand the work.

Using the liner brush and Burnt Umber, paint in the dot and comma detail in the arch frames, and the border details.

Now using the pale yellow mix and the No. 2 liner brush paint in the internal details of the knight, the shield and the dog. You can freehand this in or transfer it on with white graphite paper, perhaps adding your own details.

All the dotted work is painted with lots of texture in the pale yellow mix.

Very gently rub the edges of the lid with your finger touched into Rich Gold—you do not want a heavy gold colour.

I antiqued this piece using Burnt Sienna oil paint and absolutely no patina. Rub a light layer of oil paint over the surface for an even coverage, then using cotton buds gently rub in highlights wherever you want them; for instance, in the border of the lid design I highlighted the tips of the spear shapes. This technique gives a lovely soft gently shaded effect. When you are happy with the box, antique the inside using the normal method and Burnt Sienna oil paint.

Leave to cure and wax.

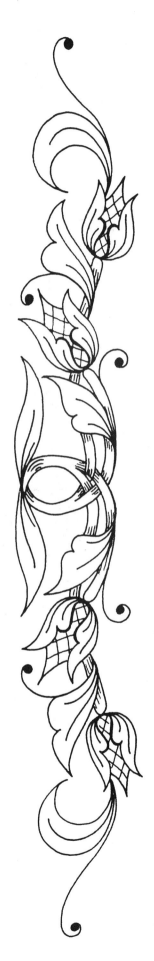

KLEISTER & RENAISSANCE DESIGN ALTERNATIVES

I painted this plate with a split personality as an exercise to show how a stencil design ideal for a Kleister project can also be painted as a less disjointed Renaissance project, with appropriate borders. Early folk artists, comfortable with the use of stencils, in this way reworked many designs. I don't suggest you should paint a plate like this—but by doubling either pattern you have a choice of two designs. Both are quick easy projects ideal for a plate or the top of a medium round cheese box. Repeat the border designs around the bands of the boxes.

KLEISTER CHEESE BOX

Pattern on page 68

Tools
Medium-sized pine cheese box,
    26.5 cm diameter x 6.5 cm (10½"
    diameter x 2½" approx.)
Base-coat brush
Stencil material
Cutting knife and mat
No. 6 stencil brush
No. 2 liner brush
Chalk pencil
Antiquing equipment
Burnt Sienna oil paint
Beeswax

Paints and mediums
Burnt Sienna
Glaze Medium
Burnt Umber
Titanium White
Yellow Oxide
Raw Sienna

Pale parchment mix = Titanium White + a touch each of Yellow Oxide and Raw Sienna.

Demonstration plate showing the same basic design worked in Kleister technique (left) and the Renaissance style (right)

Sand the box well and glaze with Burnt Sienna and glaze medium mixed in equal quantities. Allow to dry and sand lightly.

Transfer the pattern onto the stencil material twice to make a full circle. Only one repeat of the border need be cut, as a separate stencil. This is a positive stencil where paint is applied to the surface through the holes in the stencil.

Stencil in the main design using a Burnt Umber and Burnt Sienna mix (equal parts) for full coverage. Paint this colour around the border also. Dry and sand lightly.

Divide the border into four equal segments marked with chalk pencil to help you position the border stencil evenly. Using the pale parchment mix stencil the border pattern four times around the edge of the lid.

Now, using the liner brush and the pale parchment mix, outline and detail everything except the border scrolls. Add a few extra commas and dots in Burnt Umber.

Antique in Burnt Sienna oil paint and wax when cured.

RENAISSANCE CHEESE BOX

Pattern on page 69

Tools
Medium-sized pine cheese box,
   26.5 cm diameter x 6.5 cm
   (10½" diameter x 2½" approx.)
Base-coat brush
Grey and white graphite paper
Stylus
Flat brush for painting border
No. 4 round brush (or equivalent)
No. 2 liner brush
Antiquing equipment
Burnt Umber oil paint
Beeswax

Paints and mediums
Yellow Oxide
Glaze Medium
Ultramarine
Carbon Black
Naphthol Crimson
Green Oxide
Burnt Umber
Titanium White

Sand the box well and glaze with equal parts of Yellow Oxide and glaze medium. Allow to dry.

Trace the centre design twice to give a full circular pattern.

Transfer the centre design and border line (but not the scrolls in the border). Paint the border in dark blue (Ultramarine + Carbon Black) using the flat brush, then transfer the scroll detail.

Using the round brush, wash in all the colours except for the yellow areas which are left blank (not even given a second coat of yellow). Red means Naphthol Crimson, blue means Ultramarine and green means Green Oxide.

With the liner brush outline the design and paint in the Burnt Umber detail, including the small scrolls near the edge of the border.

Now add the white detail and scrolls in the border with the liner brush, texturing only the commas and the dots.

Antique using Burnt Umber oil paint and wax when cured.

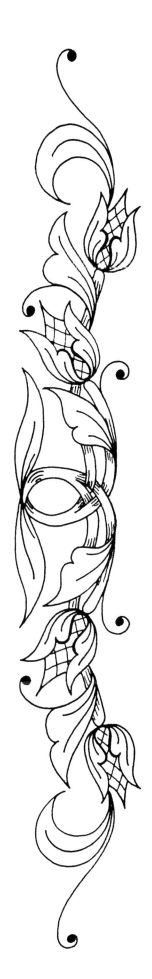

ΝΑΡΟLEΟΝ BRIDE BOX

Illustrated on page 38
Pattern on page 70

Traditional bride boxes often depicted the bride and groom, but I decided to paint another old design on this one. The lid of the box is based on a piece painted in 1800. The words around the lid, surrounding a portrait of Napoleon, translate roughly as 'I took it upon myself to go through the whole world'. The design on the side is a mixture of a number of old ideas using traditional techniques. In keeping with tradition both the inside and the underside of the box are left raw to show the quality of the wood.

Tools
Oval pine bride box,
   27 cm x 19 cm x 17 cm
   (10½″ x 7½″ x 6¾″ approx.)
Base-coat brush
Grey and white graphite paper
Stylus
No 4 round brush (or equivalent)
No. 2 liner brush
6 mm (¼″) masking tape
Antiquing equipment
Burnt Umber oil paint
Beeswax

Paints and mediums
Fawn
Carbon Black (= CB)
Brown Earth (= BE)
Red Earth (= R)
Decor Crackle Medium
Titanium White (= TW or W)
Ultramarine (= B)
Naphthol Crimson (= NC)
Yellow Oxide (= Y)
Paynes Grey
Green Oxide (= G)
Nimbus Grey

Do not sand the box before you start. Base in the top of the lid with one coat of Fawn. The sides of the lid and box are based in one coat of Carbon Black, and the inside and underside are left raw. Allow to dry and sand lightly. Onto the lid transfer just the oval border line and the line of the ground. Paint a Brown Earth wash on the ground area with the round brush. Paint the border in Red Earth. Allow to dry.

Lid Transfer all the detail on now with the No. 4 round brush. Paint crackle medium over the horse in a patchy coverage, staying away from the hooves, medallion,

Bride box in traditional oval shape features an old design of Napoleon dating from 1800

eye and mane. Allow to dry. Paint in the horse using straight Titanium White and the No. 4 round (no water). Do not overwork the horse; its coat will be a bit patchy and textured, but it can be sanded gently when dry if you wish, and a little texture makes it more interesting.

Paint in the rest of the areas smoothly, using the No. 4 round brush. For the rider's skin use Titanium White and a little Red Earth. Paint hat, boots and hooves in Carbon Black, the waistcoat in Ultramarine and the trousers in Ultramarine with a litttle Carbon Black added. Napoleon's coat is Naphthol Crimson, while the saddle blanket is Red Earth. The top of the boot is Yellow Oxide, and the hair Brown Earth. Paint the horse's mane and tail in Nimbus Grey, using textured strokes, then use the same colour on a fairly dry brush to add some shading to the horse.

With the No. 4 round brush, paint the lace at Napoleon's neck and wrists with watery Titanium White. Napoleon's eye is painted white. Change to the liner brush and paint the outline and details in Brown Earth. His lips are painted in Naphthol Crimson darkened with Brown Earth. Add the nose details and outline the skin in Brown Earth. The horse's head, mane and tail details are painted in Paynes Grey, and all the remaining outlines are painted in the same colour. Add Yellow Oxide detail to the uniform, saddle blanket, reins, medallion, spurs and hooves. Fill in the saddle blanket with watery Yellow Oxide swirls.

The lettering around the border is painted in textured Yellow Oxide with the liner brush, using strokes. By using this technique the lettering is enhanced when the box is antiqued and will appear to be painted in two shades of yellow. Textured Titanium White strokes are added to the lace, and dots to the reins and top of the boot.

Sides The floral design on the side of the box runs from left to right. On the side of the lid it is turned upside down and runs in the other direction. To transfer the design to the side of the box, start at the join line, and repeat four times, adjusting where needed. Before transferring the design to the lid, place a band of 6 mm (¼") masking tape around the bottom edge, and place a second band immediately above it. Remove the first band of tape and paint that area in Red Earth, making sure the second band of tape is firmly pressed down so no seepage can occur. When the Red Earth has dried remove the tape. This is a quick and easy way to paint a narrow trim. Now transfer the design to the side of the lid.

The large flowers are all painted in watery Red Earth using the No. 4 round brush. Use the liner brush to add the details—Yellow Oxide on the tulips and Titanium White on the round-topped flowers. The leaves are painted in Green Oxide with the No. 4 round brush, using the liner brush for the Yellow Oxide detail. The small daisies are painted in Titanium White with the No. 4 round, one stroke per petal with some texture, then give them a Yellow Oxide centre with small Naphthol Crimson dots. Use the same brush to paint the small buds in Titanium White, with texture painted with a spiral motion. The little bud stems are a Green Oxide comma starting just inside the white bud ball, using the liner brush.

The ribbon effect at the top and bottom of the sides is painted in Red Earth with the No. 4 round brush; paint alternating sections with two heavy coats and one watery coat to get the light and dark effect, with the detail painted in Yellow Oxide with the liner brush. Put the box together and run a pencil around it where the top overlaps the bottom; this will give you a finishing line for all the little white swirls in the background, painted with the liner brush. These are a traditional way of filling up background and make a very simple pattern look quite intricate; they must be watery and reasonably faint so they do not overpower the design. Fill up all the gaps on the black background but do not touch the flowers, leaves, buds or stems. The same effect is worked in Yellow Oxide on the saddle blanket.

Antique the box in Burnt Umber, on the painted surfaces only. Leave to cure and then wax.

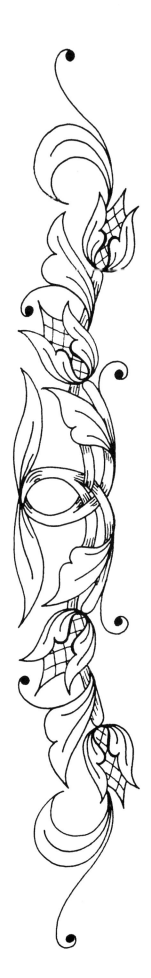

UPRIGHT SECRETAIRE

Illustrated on page 42
Pattern on page 72

This is a lovely project which looks deceptively complex. The front design with the onion domes is based on an old trunk dated 1720. The design and technique are simple, and slightly wobbly lines will not detract from the finished appeal.

Tools
Upright pine secretaire with
    drawer, 40 cm x 27 cm 16 cm
    (16" x 10½" 6¼" approx.)
Grey graphite paper
Stylus
No. 4 round brush (or equivalent)
No. 2 liner brush
25 mm (1") flat brushes for
    striped border
Antiquing equipment
Burnt Umber oil paint
Beeswax

Paints and mediums
Burgundy
Brown Earth
Burnt Umber
Glaze Medium
Yellow Oxide
Carbon Black
Green Oxide
Ultramarine
Raw Sienna (= RS)
Titanium White (= TW)

Glaze mix (GL) = 4 parts Burgundy + 4 parts Brown Earth + 1 part Burnt Umber + 8 parts glaze medium.

Green mix (GR) = 4 parts Carbon Black + 1 part Green Oxide + touch of Ultramarine.

Remove the fittings and sand all surfaces. Base all the outside surfaces and the inside of the door in one coat of Yellow Oxide. The other inside surfaces are glazed with the glaze mix. Allow to dry and sand all surfaces lightly.

Transfer all the patterns, except the little swirls and the scrolls in the stripes on the sides, top and drawer front.

Base in all the separate areas with the No. 4 round brush, using watery colours, except for the areas on the front of the secretaire marked GL, where you use the glaze mix used on the inside of the box. Base in the following order, referring to the codes on the design—glaze mix (GL), Raw Sienna (RS), white (TW) and lastly the green mix (GR); the green needs to be fairly watery to allow the yellow background to glow through.

Using the liner brush, paint all the Carbon Black outlines and detail. Paint in a few fine watery white lines in the green domes and on the yellow tiles.

Paint the black scrolls above the arch with the round brush and the S strokes in the white border areas with the liner brush. Fill in the black background swirls above and below the arch, and finally paint the white textured commas on the black scrolls.

Striped border, top, drawer and sides Using flat brushes, block in the Raw Sienna stripes, then the green mix stripes. Allow to dry and transfer the remaining details.

All the stripes are outlined in Carbon Black using the liner brush, then the black scrolls and curls are painted with the round brush.

Using the liner brush, add the dots and textured commas in Titanium White, and finally the fine watery white lines where indicated on the pattern.

The edges and base of the secretaire are painted in the green mix with a flat brush or base-coat brush.

Antique with Burnt Umber oil paint, cure and then wax.

Front and side views of upright secretaire. The oval box is described on page 27.

43

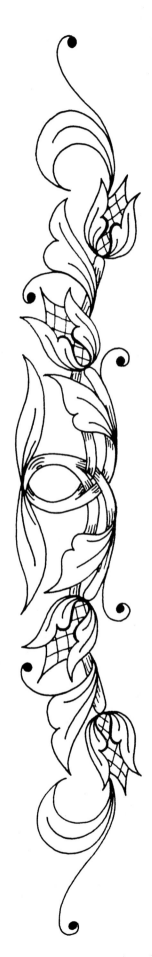

RENAISSANCE CLOCK

Pattern on page 76

I love this clock, but it requires some careful liner work and a bit of patience. My design is not strictly traditional, with its twisted interlocking leaves, but the general impression and layout is Swiss Renaissance folk art. This is a solid pine clock with extra depth to accommodate a pendulum movement.

Tools
Pine dome clock, 43 cm x 30 cm
 (17" x 12")
Base-coat brush
Grey graphite paper
Stylus
No. 2 round brush (or equivalent)
No. 4 round brush (or equivalent)
No. 2 liner brush
12 mm and 6 mm (½" and ¼") flat
 brushes for borders
Antiquing equipment
Burnt Sienna and Burnt Umber
 oil paints
Beeswax

Paints and mediums
Raw Sienna
Naphthol Crimson
Carbon Black
Green Oxide
Ultramarine
Titanium White

Sand all surfaces, then base all surfaces with one coat of Raw Sienna. Allow to dry and sand lightly.

Transfer all the pattern, except for the liner work in the two circular red bands on the dial and in the arched red border band. Wash in these red bands using a flat brush slightly narower than the band you are painting, allow to dry and then transfer the remaining details.

Base in all the colours in washy paint according to the pattern, using the No. 2 round brush for the small areas and the No. 4 round for larger areas.

Red (R) = Naphthol Crimson
Dark red (DR) = Naphthol Crimson + touch of Carbon Black
Green (G) = Green Oxide
Dark green (DG) = Green Oxide + touch of Carbon Black
Blue (B) = Ultramarine
Dark blue (DB) = Ultramarine + touch of Carbon Black

The yellow areas are not painted further; they are just the background Raw Sienna.

When you are painting the roses, paint the whole petal red, then paint the dark red turn on top; the blue petal is added last. It is easier to completely base in a shape with strokes and then add extra detail on top. Trying to paint around a shape will result in messy strokes, very visible when painting with washy colours. Paint the pale sections of the leaves first, then the dark sections. Use the No. 2 round brush for small areas and the No. 4 for larger areas.

Outline all the leaves in Carbon Black with the liner brush. Try to keep your lines fine. Then add all the details in Carbon Black.

The clock numbers are painted in Carbon Black using the No. 2 round brush.

Outline the red bands in white with the liner brush, then add all the white details to bands, flowers and leaves. Lastly add the white dots.

The trim around the outer edge of the clock is dark blue.

Antique using Burnt Sienna and a touch of Burnt Umber oil paint.

When the clock is cured either wax it, or rub with wire wool and varnish.

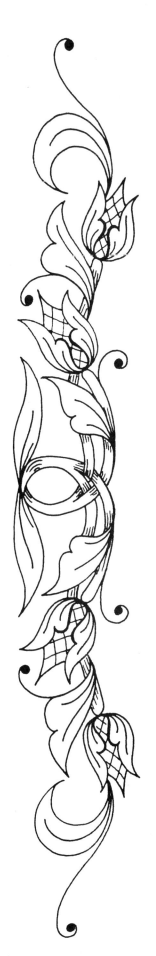

ART NOUVEAU LAP DESK

Illustrated on page 48
Pattern on page 78

I have always been interested in Art Nouveau designs, probably because they have the same simple stylisation as early folk art, often deceptively so. When you really study an Art Nouveau design you realise is is not as simple as it appeared at first glance. It was the stylisation of flowers and foliage that first gave me the idea of using the Kleister technique for this project, then taking it a step further using rather unusual colours. This is a straightforward project for anyone with cutting and liner work experience. The lap desk is craftwood, quite a bit bigger than most available, and has a sliding drawer inside to keep pens in.

Tools
Large craftwood lap desk,
   38 cm x 35 cm x 13 cm
   (15″ x 13¾″ x 5″ approx.)
Base-coat brush
Grey graphite paper
Stylus
Masking film
Cutting knife
Small sea sponge
No. 2 liner brush
Small flat brush for trim
Plastic wrap
Antiquing equipment
Burnt Umber oil paint
Beeswax

Paints and mediums
Damask Rose (base-coat paint)
Deep Plum (base-coat paint)
Decor Crackle Medium
Kleister Medium
Carbon Black
Burnt Umber

Remove all fittings and base in the desk with three or four coats of Damask Rose, sanding after each coat. All surfaces should be smooth. The outside must have a complete coverage of paint, but coverage of the inside is not so critical as a second technique will be used over it.

Art Nouveau lap desk

Transfer all the designs onto the lid and sides of the lap desk. Lay the masking film over all sides and the top and mask out all the leaves and the whole flower (the darker part of the flower is painted in later). Make sure all cut edges of the film are pressed down well before you continue. You are removing the film from the dark background areas, leaving the flowers and leaves covered.

Using a sea sponge that has been dampened and squeezed out really well, apply the crackle medium thickly to all the outside surfaces, except for the routed trim and the pen groove. If you get a bit of crackle on those areas, wipe it up straight away. I also crackled the inside of the lid and the inner pen tray. When the crackle medium seems dry, wait another one or two hours, then sponge on the Deep Plum using only enough water in the sponge to make it slightly damp (almost no water at all). Again clean up the groove and trim immediately.

Allow to dry and sand lightly. This will give you a smoother surface and show up the edges of the film, making for easier removal. Carefully remove the film. If both the paint and the crackle are very thick, give another light sand to enable you to outline the design.

Mix equal parts of Deep Plum and Kleister medium and gently dab in the shaded areas on the flower, using a small flat or round brush. This same mix is used inside the lap desk, using plastic wrap instead of the brush. While it is still wet dab the crumpled plastic wrap on it to give a marbled effect.

Outline the designs in Carbon Black with the liner brush, adding a few commas in the base of the flower. Great care needs to be taken with the liner work in this design. It should be well done and flowing, as the design is so simple that the liner work is really obvious.

Using the small flat brush paint the routed trim in Burnt Umber.

Antique in Burnt Umber oil paint and wax when cured.

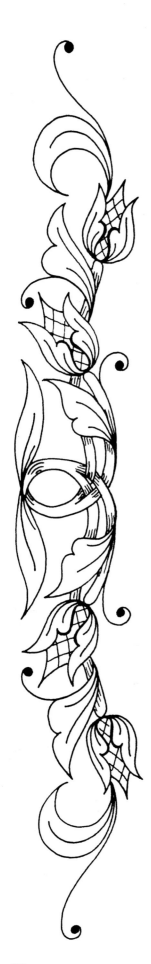

INLAY FIRE SCREEN

Pattern on page 50

Although the original inspiration for this design came when I was looking through a book of fretwork designs for scroll saws, the end result reflects very little of that source. I wanted the screen to look like very fine wood inlay. This is a reasonably demanding project involving a lot of cutting and fine liner work. The shadows on the scrolls are created during the antiquing process. A small section of the pattern is repeated on the back of the screen.

Tools
Craftwood screen, 60 cm
   (24") square
Base-coat brush
Grey graphite paper
Stylus
Masking film
Cutting knife
Masking tape
Hogshair brush
No. 8 stencil brush
No. 4 round brush (or equivalent)
No. 2 liner brush
Antiquing equipment
Burnt Sienna and Burnt Umber oil
   paint
Varnish

Paints and mediums
Raw Sienna
Kleister Medium
Burnt Sienna
Burgundy
Burnt Umber
Titanium White
Retarder

Unscrew the feet from the screen and base all surfaces in Raw Sienna, using as many coats as necessary for a full coverage. Sand after each coat for a smooth surface.

Make a full tracing of the design (refer to notes on patterns on page 13). Accuracy is the secret to this design. To start with, transfer the designs on the feet and the edges of the frame, and the inner and outer scrolls marked 1. These areas will remain unpainted. Mark on the quarter lines at the same time. The wood-grained areas

marked 2 on the main design are painted first, so mask out the scrolls and the patterns on the feet and frame, making sure the cut edges of the masking film are pressed down firmly.

Mix 4 parts Kleister medium to 1 part Burnt Sienna (this is a very transparent mix). Work on one quarter of the screen at a time, masking along the quarter lines with masking tape. Be very careful when you remove the tape to work on the next section that you do not remove or stretch the masking film covering the scrolls. On each section, paint on the Kleister mix and with the hogshair brush pull a grain line from the centre straight out to the corner, through the middle of the section; all wood-grains in this section will be parallel to this line.

The areas marked 3 are worked with a stencil brush twist. Mix Burnt Sienna and Burgundy to make a rosewood colour, dabble the mix with Kleister medium and add a few drops of retarder; this makes it easier to play with on such large areas. Working on one patch at a time, paint on the mix with a No. 8 stencil brush, then twist, overlapping the twists. The border and feet are also painted like this. Join the grain in the corners of the border at an angle of 45° to give a mitred effect, using masking tape and working one side at a time. Remove all film and sand lightly, being especially careful on the medallion area, where any texture could allow seepage.

Transfer all remaining detail accurately, not forgetting the small detail at the top of the border. Cover the centre of the screen and the top frame with masking film, which will be removed in a series of small sections.

Cut and remove the areas marked 4. Mix 1 part Burnt Sienna to 1 part Kleister medium with a touch of Burnt Umber, and wood-grain these areas in the same direction as the grain showing beneath them, using the hogshair brush.

Now remove the areas marked 5 and with the same mix repeat the procedure as for the areas marked 4.

Cut and remove areas marked 6; using a No. 4 round brush wash these areas in Burgundy.

Cut and remove areas marked 7 and paint in solid Burnt Umber with the No. 4 round brush.

Cut and remove areas marked 8; these are painted the same as the areas marked 6.

Now remove all the rest of the film. It is dangerous to leave film stuck to a project for too long, so the centre design is best completed in no more than one or two days, especially during hot weather.

Paint Burnt Umber in the groove around the edges with the No. 4 round brush.

The Burnt Umber design elements (7) are outlined in *fine* white lines with the liner brush; all other outlining, the twists on the scrolls and the four joins in the background wood-graining are painted in Burnt Umber with the liner brush.

To antique the screen use Burnt Sienna oil paint and little or no patina to start with; add some Burnt Umber to create shadows on the scrolls, gently blending out to give a soft curve to the scrolls. You may need a little patina to rub highlights to the head of each scroll. The scrolls should end up with a soft three-dimensional effect.

Leave the work to cure, then varnish.

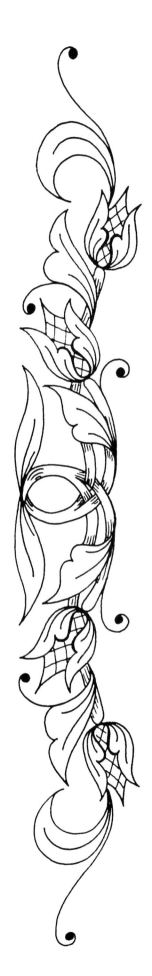

ROUND KLEISTER TRAY

Illustrated on pages 2 and 54
Pattern on page 82

This was a fairly intense project based on an ornate Victorian stencil and the result may be a little over the top for some tastes. If you prefer, either the floral medallion or the stencil inlay could be omitted. Cutting the stencil requires patience and accuracy but I really enjoyed it. In keeping with the design the wood-grains are fine and reasonably subtle.

Tools
Large craftwood tray, 45 cm x 42 cm
    (17¾" 16½" approx.)
Grey graphite paper
Stylus
Masking film
Masking tape
Hogshair brush
Base-coat brush
Stencil material
Cutting knife and mat
No. 8 stencil brush
No. 4 stencil brush
12 mm (½") flat brush
No. 4 round brush
No. 2 liner brush
Antiquing equipment
Burnt Umber and Burnt Sienna
    oil paints
Varnish

Paints and mediums
Primrose (base-coat paint)
Burnt Sienna
Kleister Medium
Burnt Umber
Burgundy
Raw Sienna
Raw Umber
Green Oxide
Glaze Medium
Carbon Black

Base all surfaces with three or four coats of Primrose, sanding after each coat. This design needs a very smooth complete coverage.

Transfer the lines marked A and the flower detail in the centre medallion (main lines only).

Cover the flower panel and lip of the tray with masking film so you can paint the wood-grain panels.

Each section of the eight sections of wood-grain is done separately, using masking tape along the 'joins' in the grain. Make up two pots of Kleister mix, one with equal parts of Burnt Umber and Kleister medium, the other with equal parts of Burnt Sienna and Kleister medium. Apply the two colours randomly to the section you are working on, then stroke in the wood-grain using the hogshair brush. You will get subtle colour variations in each section. *Note*: Pull the first wood-grain stroke from the centre of the tray through the middle of the section, then run all other strokes in this section parallel to the first stroke. Working like this will create realistic 'joins' between the sections. Make sure there are no gaps between the sections; in fact, it is better if they overlap slightly. Remove all the masking film when all eight sections have been wood-grained.

Trace the stencil pattern onto the stencil material, repeating it for the second side, as recommended in the notes on stencilling on page 16. Cut the stencil, referring again to the stencilling notes. Stencil the pattern onto the wood-grain sections, sanding lightly before stencilling if you have a lot of texture in this area. Use the No. 8 stencil brush and a rosewood mix of Burnt Umber and Burgundy (I leave the proportions to your preference). Make sure the wood-grain is well covered before you carefully remove the stencil.

The next step is to paint the band just inside the lip of the tray. Mask over the stencilled area. Mix one part each Burnt Umber and Burnt Sienna with two parts Kleister medium. Base in small areas with this mix and twist the No. 4 stencil brush into the based area, allowing the twists to touch and slightly overlap in places. Clean off any Kleister mix that gets into the lip of the tray, wiping it off as you go around. Any textured Kleister would spoil the smooth finish of the edge. When all the band is painted remove the masking film.

With the liner brush paint a thin Carbon Black line between the 'twist' area and the stencilled area, to cover the join.

Paint the lip and the base of the tray in the rosewood stencil mix. You will need at least two coats. You may still end up with some lighter patches, but if you base in the direction of a wood-grain they can add to your wood-grain effect. Lightly sand all rosewood areas including the stencilling. Now using a 12 mm (½") flat brush and Burnt Umber, float a very subtle, fairly straight wood-grain onto the lip and the base of the tray. Remember to keep the grain going always from the centre of the tray to the edge.

Wash in the flowers now with the No. 4 round brush, following the codes on the pattern:
Red (R) = Burgundy + Burnt Umber
Orange (O) = Burgundy + Raw Sienna
Yellow (Y) = Raw Sienna
Green (G) = Raw Sienna + Green Oxide in varying proportions

The centres of the rose and the lily-type flower are painted Burnt Umber. Outline and detail the flowers in Burnt Umber using very fine strokes with your liner brush. Erase any visible graphite lines.

Mask around the flower panel so you can float a wood-grain through it. Mix equal parts of Burnt Sienna and glaze medium and with extra glaze medium in a 12 mm (½") flat brush float the glaze mix straight through the flower panel, over the flowers; this will protect the washes when antiquing. Remove masking and outline flower panel in Carbon Black with the liner brush.

Antique the tray in Burnt Umber and Burnt Sienna, rubbing some highlights into the flowers.

Leave to cure and then varnish.

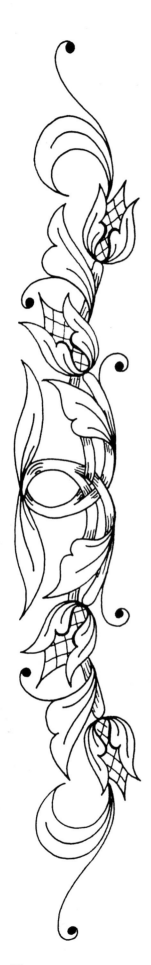

ALPBACHTAL MEDICINE CUPBOARD

Pattern on page 84

This is a really traditional project, scaled down for a small pine medicine cabinet complete with shelves and a drawer inside. My design is a composite based on three cupboards all dating from the eighteenth century, from Alpbach in the region of the Tyrol in Austria. A lot of the design was constructed using a compass and ruler in the traditional way. I used a limited palette of red, green, black and white; the yellow (Raw Sienna) background, while not counted as a colour, is used to seal the wood. After antiquing the background will simulate mellow aged wood. The project requires some patience and good liner work because the design is relatively small.

Tools
Pine cupboard,
    55 cm x 39 cm x 21 cm
    (21½" 15½" x 8¼" approx.)
Base-coat brush
Grey graphite paper
Stylus
Pencil and ruler
No. 2 round brush (or equivalent)
No. 2 liner brush
12 mm (½") flat brush
Antiquing equipment
Burnt Umber oil paint
Beeswax

Paints and mediums
Raw Sienna (base-coat)
Yellow Oxide
Carbon Black
Norwegian Orange (= R)
Titanium White

Dark green mix (G) = Yellow Oxide + enough Carbon Black to make a good dark green.

Remove all fittings from the cupboard and sand all surfaces, especially the cut edges and corners. Base all surfaces in one coat of Raw Sienna and sand when dry.

Transfer all the designs. On the sides of the cupboard and inside the doors I ruled a 2 cm (¾") border all around, then centred the motif.

All colours are painted in watery paint with the No. 2 round brush.

Using the dark green mix (G), paint in all the leaves and green scrolls.

Using Norwegian Orange (R) paint in the flowers and main stems, the circles and the twists inside them, the central shapes and the small scrolls around the centre motif on the doors and the twists inside (repeated on the sides and the inner surface of the doors).

Base in all the white (W) areas next, following the code on the design. The petals of the daisies in the corners of the designs are painted as little spirals.

The striping around the edges of the doors and the sides of the panels is painted next. Keep it muted and random. Double load the 12 mm (½") flat with Norwegian Orange and the dark green mix and pull single strokes out to the edges. Stripe the 'thickness' of the doors and a band around the insides of the doors as well, as shown in the photograph. Create a mitre in each corner by striping at a 45° angle at the corner. This will be tidied up with liner work later.

The outer trim is painted in the dark green mix, following the photograph. Paint the knobs for the doors and the drawer as well, and the edges of the shelves.

Using the liner brush, outline all the elements of the design in Carbon Black. Also paint in the minor stems and curls, adding the black dots in the corners of the motifs and the black strokes in the central areas of the scrolls.

The white detail is mostly painted in watery Titanium White with the liner brush, using texture only in the dots and commas. Paint in the white daisies on the green trim around the doors. The drawer detail is painted in the same way.

Antique with Burnt Umber oil paint and wax when cured.

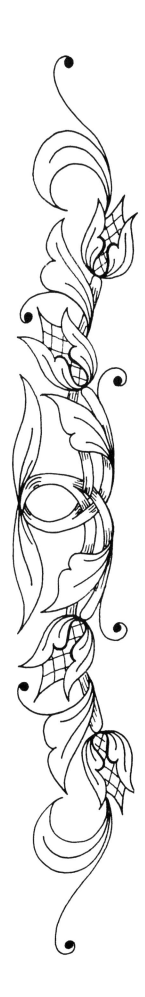

BiBLiOGRAPhy

Brandt, Diana: *The Rustic Charm of Folk Art*, Text Publishing Company Pty Ltd, Melbourne 1992

Droge, Kurt: *Bemalte Spanschachteln*, Lothar Pretzell, George D.W. Callwey, Munich 1986, ISBN 3-7667-1812-0

Lipp, Franz C.: *Öber Ostereichische Bauern Möbel*, Kremayr & Scheriau, Vienna 1986, ISBN 3-218-00428-4

von Merhart, Nenna: *Bauernmöbel Malerei*, George D.W. Callwey, Munich 1986, ISBN 3-7667-0809-0

Norris, Malcolm: *Brass Rubbing*, Studio Vista, London 1965, republished Pan Books, London 1977, ISBN 0-330-25095-7

Spero, James: *Decorative Pattern from Historic Sources*, Dover Publications Inc., New York 1986, ISBN 0-486-25120-9

SMALL RECTANGULAR KLEISTER BOX

(page 22)

LID

SIDE

SIDE

small oval kleister box
(*page 23*)

LID

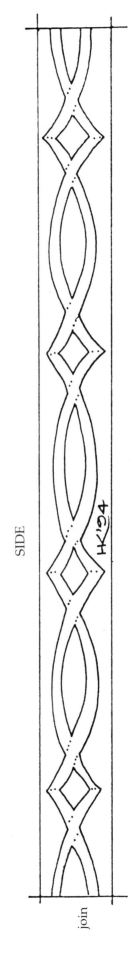

SIDE

join

61

medium kleister & renaissance tulip box

(page 26)

ENLARGE AT 125%
(4 cm = 5 cm; 2″ = 2½″)

LID

SIDE

SIDE

MEDIUM OVAL RENAISSANCE BOX

(page 27)

ENLARGE AT 125%
(4 cm = 5 cm; 2" = 2½")

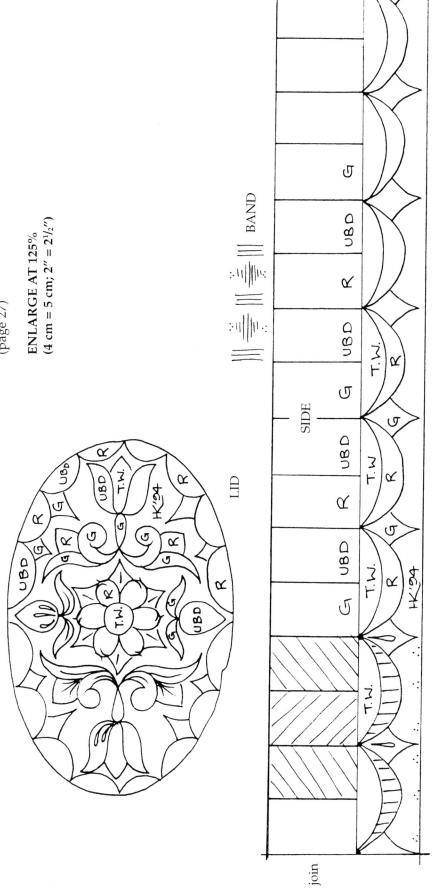

LID

SIDE

BAND

join

LARGE OVAL ALPBACHTAL BOX

(page 30)

ACTUAL SIZE

LID

join

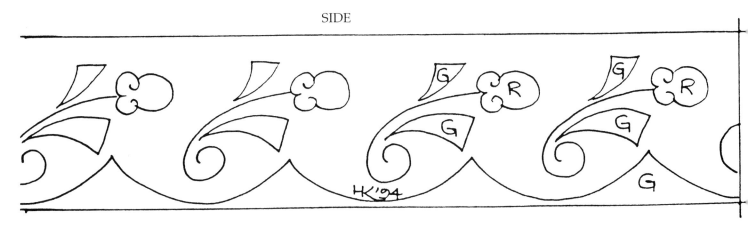

BRASS RUBBING BOX

(page 32)

ACTUAL SIZE

DETAIL

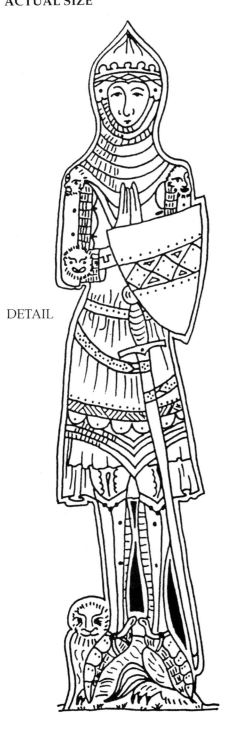

LID

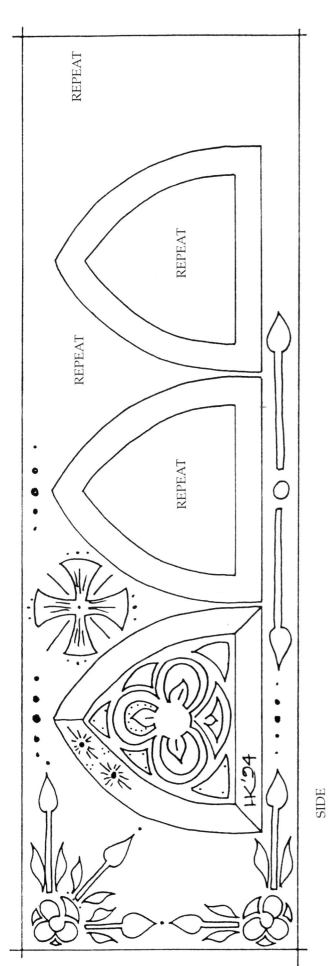

SIDE

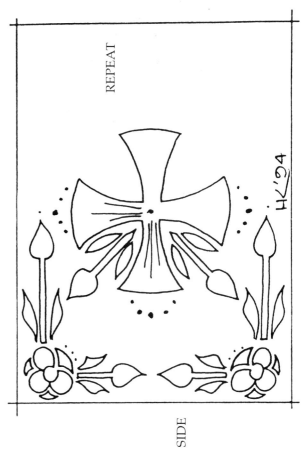

SIDE

67

KLEiSTER CHEESE BOX
(page 34)

ACTUAL SIZE

HK'94

RENAISSANCE
CHEESE BOX
(page 36)

ACTUAL SIZE

69

DAPOLEOD BRIDE BOX

(page 37)

ACTUAL SIZE

SIDE

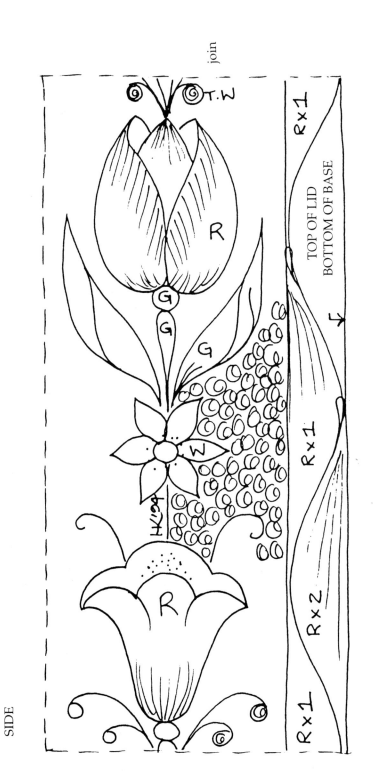

join

T.W

R

G

G

G

W

high

R

R×1

R×1

R×2

R×1

TOP OF LID

BOTTOM OF BASE

70

LID

upright secretaire (front)

(page 41)

ENLARGE AT 125%
(4 cm = 5 cm; 2″ = 2½″)

GR RS GR RS GR RS RS

TW

T.W. GL GL

GR GL GL

T.W. GL GL GL

RS

GR GL TW GL GR GL

GR RS GR RS

GL TW

join

72

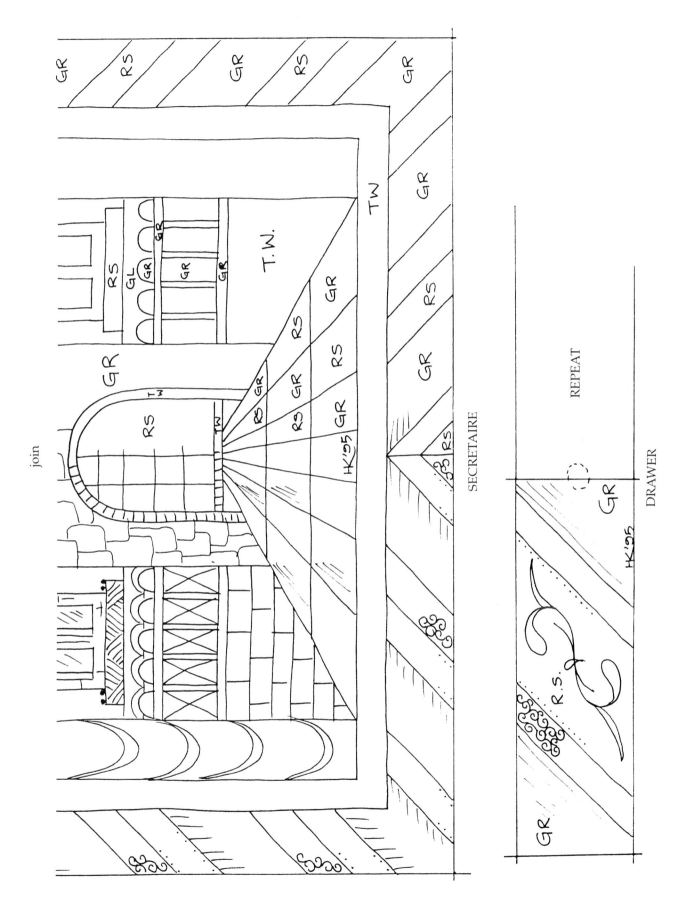

join

SECRETAIRE

REPEAT

DRAWER

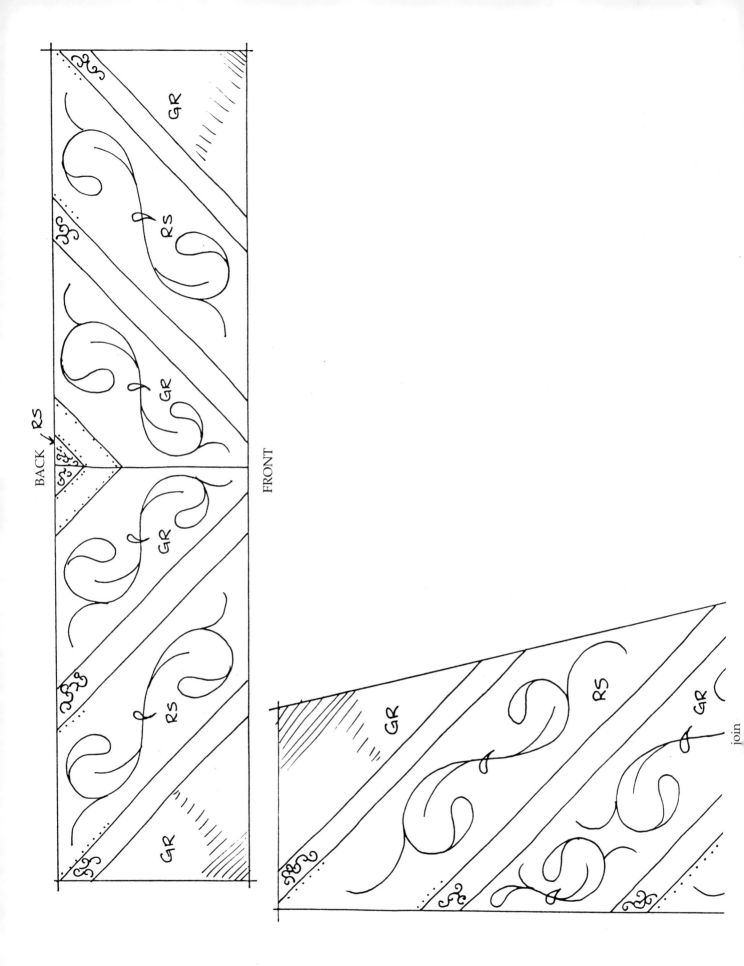

BACK

RS

GR

RS

GR

GR

GR

RS

GR

FRONT

GR

RS

GR

join

upright secretaire
[side & top]
(page 41)

ENLARGE AT 125%
(4 cm = 5 cm; 2" = 2½")

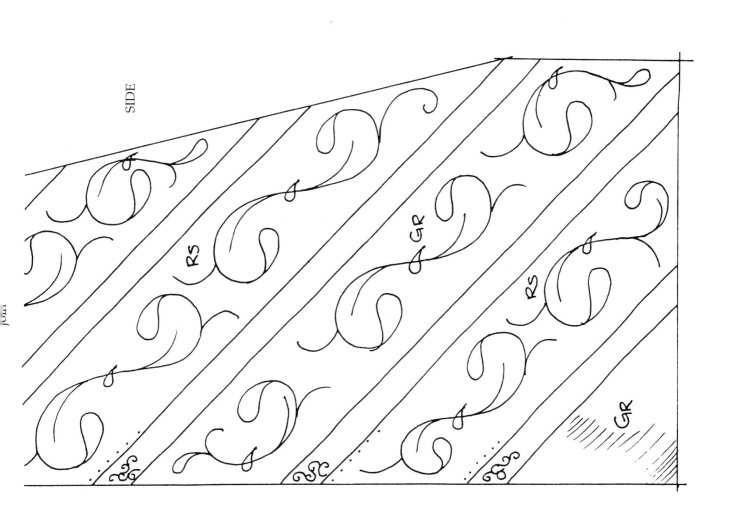

SIDE

RS

GR

RS

GR

RENAISSANCE CLOCK
(page 44)

ENLARGE AT 125%
(4 cm = 5 cm; 2″ = 2¹⁄₂″)

ART NOUVEAU
LAP DESK
(page 47)

ENLARGE AT 125%
(4 cm = 5 cm; 2″ = 2½″)

CENTRE LINE

REPEAT AS FOR
RIGHT SIDE

LAP DESK LID

HK'95

PEN GROOVE

TOP OF LAP DESK
FRONT SIDE
BACK SIDE

LAP DESK SIDES

inlay fire screen

(page 50)

ENLARGE AT 125%
(4 cm = 5 cm; 2" = 2½")

FEET

TOP

¾ line

join

−¼ line

join

AND BOTTOM

TOP
FRAME

join

join

join

FRAME SIDES

BOTTOM

¼ line

HK'94

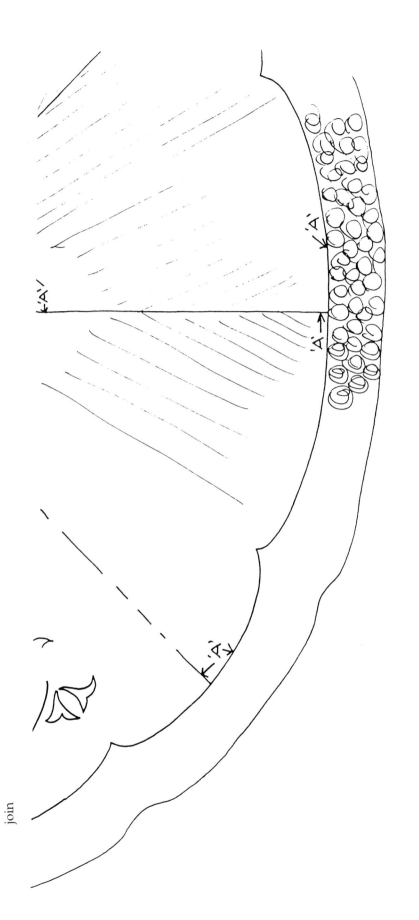

join

Round
Kleister tray
(page 53)

ENLARGE AT 125%
(4 cm = 5 cm; 2″ = 2½″)

FRONT TOP

ALPBACHTAL
MEDICINE CUPBOARD
(page 56)

ENLARGE AT 125%
(4 cm = 5 cm; 2″ = 2½″)

DRAWER SIDE

DRAWER FRONT AND BACK

SIDE TOP

MOTIF FOR SIDES AND
INSIDE DOORS

REPEAT TOP PANEL

BOTH DOORS THE SAME

index